Greetings & Salutations

Hi and hello are both common words that are used when meeting and greeting one another. I think it is safe to assume that most of you are familiar with the greetings; Bonjour, Good Morning, Assalamualaikum, Ohayou Gozaimasu, amongst the many other greeting words from different countries and cultures around the world. Here, we are going to talk about how we greet one another on the island of Bali, also known as The Last Paradise, The Land of a Thousand Temples, and The Morning of the World. When you first arrive on the island, almost all Balinese people will put their palms together in front of their chest with their fingertips pointing up. In doing this, Balinese people will say "Om Swastiastu". Every place in Bali will most likely welcome you by this sentence. This sentence comes from Sanskrit, an ancient Indo-European language of India, used in Hindu scriptures, and is thus commonly used in daily communication, as well as in Hindu prayers on Bali. The word anatomy of Om Swastiastu is broken down into its meanings below;

Om means God, who goes by the name of Sang Hyang Widhi in Bali.

Su (written as Swa) means good, well, nice, great, or right.

Asti means there, and Astu means hope.

The overall meaning of Om Swastiatu resides within peacefulness. Om Swastiastu essentially means good luck with God's grace, and it is with this greeting that we channel positive energy to one another here in Bali. When said to another person, this sentence expresses a prayer for protection by God, and harmonious co-habitation with all living beings. This is because in Hinduism, respect is highly important when it comes to maintaining good relationships, and reducing disputes between humans as well as other living creatures. Most ways of greeting in Bali are given in the form of prayers.

If you are wondering what the appropriate response might be to Om Swasiastu, it is common to reply also with Om Swasiastu, although it is not mandatory. It is a peaceful beginning to an exchange of ideas, and one of the many tranquilities found on the island of Bali.

Hindus are always taught to say good words and to bless others with good things. Thus, brings us to talk about the meaning of Om Santih Santih Santih Om. Every beginning has an ending. In this context, Om Swastiastu begins a connection between people, and is therefore ended with the words; Om Santih Santih Santih Om. This phrase is explained below;

Om means God, as mentioned above.

Santih means peace.

This closing sentence essentially means; may you be safe and may peace be in your heart, may peace be on earth, and may peace be always. Another simple way of expressing this particular intention is to say; God bless you!

Now, you already know two common sentences that are often heard in Bali. Every sentence that we say will always bring peaceful intentions.

- Triana Ardi

Publisher
Earth Afloat Publishing

Art Director & Executive Editor
Thirumoolar Devar

Associate Editor
Kayli Wouters

Administration
Farin Mufarohah

Writers
Kayli Wouters
Triana Ardi
Allison Moore
Thirumoolar Devar

Translation
Kayli Wouters
Farin Mufarohah

Illustrator
Ngrh Yudha

InDesign Layout & Ad Production
Thirumoolar Devar

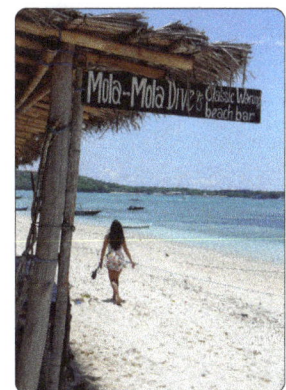

Cover Shot: @earthafloat
When in Nusa Lembongan you can visit Mola Mola and the Classic Warung at the far end of Jungutbatu Beach to see this view!

HowToBali.com
Producer
Thirumoolar Devar

Programming
Fery Satria Kristianto

Graphic Design
Valencia Huang

Earth Afloat Publishing
© Copyright 2023
English Edition
ISBN: 978-1-7353953-6-4

look inside

Bali Terrestrial & Aquatic

Birth of an Island

Home to some of the world's deepest ocean trenches and abundant terrestrial and marine biodiversity, Indonesia is also known for its rich and intense history of natural disasters; consisting of powerful volcanic eruptions, devastating tsunamis, and mighty earthquakes.

photo: @alitsuarnegara

Served on a Plate

The Indonesian archipelago is one of the most seismically active locations on planet Earth. Situated on the boundary of several major tectonic plates, and forming part of the Pacific Ring of Fire. Forging over 300 million years, the some 17,000 Indonesian islands are the result of movement between four primary tectonic plates. These include the Indo-Australian Plate, the Eurasian Plate, the Caroline Plate and the Philippine Sea Plate. Subduction, convergence and transformative movements between these plates are responsible for the vast number of island arcs, volcanoes, earthquakes and trenches that combine to create the beauty and authenticity of Indonesia.

The Land is Alive!

The island of Bali emerged due to tectonic subduction. This occurs when one tectonic plate descends below another as they collide at their boundaries. Bali was formed through the subduction of the Indo-Australian Plate under the Eurasian Plate. At the time of subduction, the ocean floor was composed of marine deposits, coral reefs and layers of limestone, which were lifted above sea level as a result of this movement. Thus, the geological makeup of Bali is divided by a string of mountains and volcanoes, ranging from the East to the West of the Northern half of the island. The land surrounding the volcanoes consist of volcanic soils and black sand beaches, whilst the regions of Bali's Southern peninsula consist mainly of limestone and white sand, being farther away from the volcanoes of the island.

Bali is home to three main volcanoes; Mount Agung, Mount Batur and Mount Batukaru. The highest point of the island lies on the summit of Mount Agung at 3,142 meters above sea level[1]. Combined with tropical weather and bountiful amounts of rainfall, regions surrounding the volcanoes are rich with nutrients and volcanic soil

[1] Bali Fact." Bali Fact - Bali History, Geography, People. Culture and More, 2004, https://www.bali-go-round.com/bali-fact.htm.

obtained and layered from past eruptions. This geological blessing has gifted Bali with fertile land and agricultural prosperity.

Rice farming has been the main form of traditional agriculture throughout the course of the island's history. All along the

Bali also shelters many different species of terrestrial fauna, including lizards, monkeys, snakes, squirrels and over 300 species of birds.

slopes of Bali's volcanoes and mountains, rice terraces scatter the landscape. The springs that descend from the mountain lakes provide a natural source of water flow for irrigation in these terraces. A traditional form of rice farming called 'Subak' occurs in Bali. Subak is an agricultural organization of Balinese rice field farmers who manage the irrigation of their water supply. Together, they maintain canals and systems which regulate rice planting, along with distribution of water across the rice terraces[2].

In addition to farming for rice in the dry season, the wet season brings about

[2] Pratt, Daniel. "Subak - a Sustainable System of Irrigation." The Bali Retirement Villages, The Bali Retirement Villages, 16 Dec. 2016, https://thebaliv-illages.com/Bali-news/2016/10/18/subak-a-sustain-able-system-of-irrigation.

photo: @earthafloat
TheIntenseCalm.com

diversification of crops. These changes however, are not limited to; corn, barley, banana, papaya, mango, and pineapple farming, amongst a vast variety of other vegetables and fruits. In addition to rice, fruits and vegetables, the fertile land of Bali also allows the growth of coffee and cacao, a diverse array of herbs and spices, as well as numerous vibrant species of flora.

Being a lush and plentiful land of plants, it is bound to be that Bali also shelters many different species of terrestrial fauna, some of which includes lizards, monkeys, snakes and squirrels. Not to mention, more than 300 species of birds alone can be found to inhabit the skies and lands of Bali.

photo: @earthafloat
TheIntenseCalm.com

photo:
@mavis_bali

Diving Down

Famous for its magnificent compositions and epic natural sights on land, Indonesia's oceans are equally, if not, more monumental in composition and structure. Consisting of extensive underwater shelves, deep-sea basins, abyssal trenches and submarine volcanoes, Indonesia also offers one of the world's most vibrant and biodiverse marine ecosystems known to date. Located in between the Pacific and Indian Ocean, Indonesia also comprises a major part of the world's Coral Triangle. Containing approximately 67% of global coral species, and 37% of the world's coral reef fish species, Indonesia holds the largest diversity of coral reef fish on the planet[3]. In addition to coral reefs, much of the Indonesian coastline is rich with various marine ecosystems such as sea grass, mangroves, estuarial beaches and algal beds.

Specifically when zooming in on the island of Bali, the most abundant and lively coral reefs reside off the coast of neighboring islands; Nusa Penida, Nusa Ceningan and Nusa Lembongan. Amongst housing an ample diversity of coral reef fish, these three islands are distinctly visited by reef manta rays, various species of pelagic sharks, and the elusive sunfish. Being an archipelagic nation, the animals and plants of the ocean surrounding Indonesia provide a major source of human sustenance and livelihood. Unfortunately, natural marine resources are depleting due to unregulated overfishing, marine pollution, coral bleaching, sea level rise and global climate change.

Both Indonesia's land and sea have seen colossal and epic transformations over its geological history. Its rich terrestrial and marine biodiversity have occurred as a result, making Indonesia and Bali especially, an enticing and naturally wonderful place to exist.

- Kayli Wouters

[3] "8 Facts about Indonesia's Ocean | UNDP in Indonesia." United Nations Development Program, https://www.id.undp.org/content/indonesia/en/home/presscenter/articles/2016/06/08/8-facts-about-indonesia-s-ocean.html.

photo: @alitsuarnegara
pixabay.com/es/users/alitdesign-4593555/

PURI SANTRIAN
a beach resort & spa

Beach Resort & Spa

Cultivating Chocolate

The mural instantly caught my eye. "Who's that?" I asked. Alit chuckled and replied, "The best cacao was previously reserved for the king. Now, we all can eat pure chocolate like royalty."

Here's his story of how he came to start Cau Chocolate and the life-changing journey that follows...

HowToBali: Hi! Thank you for talking to us. When did you start Cau, and what lead you to creating Cau?

Alit: I am an extension agricultural worker at the Agricultural Technology Assessment Center (BPTP) in Denpasar, Bali. Working as an experienced farmer for more than 35 years, my main job is with assisting local farmers in developing their farming businesses so that they can provide good income to meet their family's needs for life, school and various social activities.

Working in agriculture, it was very difficult to increase the farmers' income. This is caused by many factors, such as pest invasions on crops and extremely cheap crop prices during the harvest season. Additionally, the prices of agricultural production inputs such as fertilizers and pesticides tend to increase over time. In the end, the sustained welfare of farmers, which is the goal of agricultural extension, seems only but a dream.

After I examined it carefully, it turned out that the farmers' needs were very simple. Namely, how they could sell their crops at a decent price, so as to gain sufficient profit. The point is an economic value that is feasible for farmers to receive.

The economic value for agricultural products is in the downstream sector, while farmers work in the upstream sector.

Therefore, it requires serious attention. How can we ensure that higher economic value in the downstream (off farm) can be enjoyed or received by farmers who work upstream (on farm).

Due to this issue, I founded the company PT. Cau Coklat Internasional, which processes cocoa beans produced by local farmers.

In undertaking this project, I can still do my job or profession as an agricultural extension worker, to guide farmers in producing good cocoa beans according to the standards set by us in the company, and to ensure that we buy the cocoa beans at a good price, thus providing good income for the cocoa farmers.

HowToBali: Are you organic and what does "organic" mean?

Alit: Yes.... I focus on developing organic chocolate. Cau Chocolate is triple certified, meeting standards set by USA, EU, and Indonesia.

Coincidentally, my Master's and doctoral studies are in Natural Resources and Environment Management. I graduated from IPB University Bogor. I understand some of how our current environmental conditions are, especially how modern forms of agriculture impact the environment and human health. The damage to our environment is constantly getting worse, and it is very disturbing to human health. One of the reasons for this damage is the increasing use of synthetic chemicals in agricultural cultivation systems (such as in fertilizers and growth hormones) which in turn causes the food from agricultural products that we consume to be unhealthy.

This is why I focus on developing organic farming, specifically organic cocoa. The development of organic cocoa provides many advantages, including; 1) Reducing the use of synthetic chemicals in agricultural cultivation systems; 2) In turn, reducing the cost of agricultural production; 3) The agricultural products produced are healthy, due to reduced residues of toxic chemicals; 4) The environment (soil, water, air) is also getting healthier; 5) The price of agricultural products produced by farmers will be more expensive; 6) People who consume it are also getting healthier; amongst many other advantages.

As chocolate entrepreneurs producing organic chocolate, we will be able to provide healthy chocolate products for consumers. No organic chocolate will be produced by a chocolate processing company, without using organic cocoa beans. We know that cocoa beans we use are produced by local cocoa farmers. Thus, the cooperation between PT. Cau Coklat Internasional and cocoa farmers must work well and harmoniously.

Organic farming is essentially a process for producing agricultural products using an organic cultivation system.

"Sustainable farming means an agricultural system that does not destroy nature. Organic farming is a form of sustainable farming. The organic farming system is very much in harmony with the Balinese philosophy. Such as Tri Hita Karana, which means to have happiness through three ways. These are:

What does "sustainable" mean?

1. Harmony between humans and humans;

2. Harmony between humans and nature (one of which is through organic farming); and

3. Harmony between humans and God Almighty."

Alit: In addition to being in harmony with Balinese life philosophy, organic farming is also one of the practices of the community, especially farmers, in saving the environment so that we can still pass it on to our children and grandchildren in good condition (not damaged). Organic farming, apart from being a sustainable agricultural practice, will also provide better yields and income to farmers as producers over time.

HowToBali: What do think about local artisanal products, both from perspectives re: commercial/branding, other competition, and a unified goal for Bali?

Alit: Artisanal chocolate has become widely known and produced by several manufacturers. In general, artisan products, especially chocolate, have a certain market segment, as they currently tend to be sold at higher prices than regular chocolate. For ordinary people, it is relatively difficult to distinguish artisanal chocolate from non-artisanal/regular chocolate.

As we know, agricultural products produced by farmers will be greatly influenced by various environmental factors depending on where and when they are produced. For example in Bali, there is little difference in taste between the cocoa beans produced by farmers in the districts of Tabanan, Buleleng, Jemberana and other areas. However, this taste will not appear if there is no good and correct process in producing chocolate, such as the process of fermentation and roasting, amongst others.

From a general commercial point of view, artisanal chocolate has yet to make a strong impact because producers and consumers are still very limited. It takes continuous effort to brand artisanal products, especially those related to local culture.

HowToBali: I find that working to attain our goals changes us. If you think back to when Cau was just an idea, and compare that to now, how do you feel you have evolved as a person?

Alit: Firstly, I feel very grateful because I can help farmers, especially cocoa farmers in Bali, to: 1) Produce healthy food products; 2) Generate better income; And 3) Contribute to saving the environment.

I am more and more confident now that if we want to do something with a good purpose, we can do it. Even though the journey until now was not easy and there were many obstacles, both internal and external.

HowToBali: Why does chocolate melt in my hand?

Alit: Good chocolate will melt at 37°C. We know that a healthy and normal human body temperature is 37°C. So if chocolate melts in your hand, it proves that the chocolate is real, of good quality, and made through a high grade manufacturing process. Therefore, to eat good chocolate, you don't need to chew it, but just to put it in your mouth and the chocolate will melt on its own, and you can eat it right away.

Speaking w/ Dr. Ir. I Wayan Alit Artha Wiguna
Interview and photos by Thirumoolar Devar

Cau Chocolates

THE CUBE SEAWEED PROJECT

Sourced from an interview with Nusa Lembongan local, I Wayan Dollar Doru

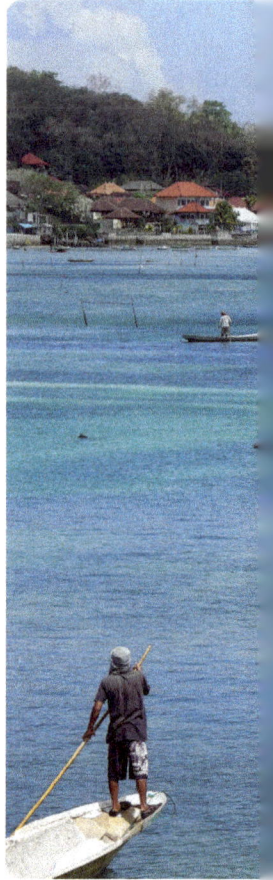

A timeline of seaweed farming

The last four decades have seen a rapid expansion, sudden halt, and slow revival of seaweed farming on the islands of Lembongan, Ceningan and Penida. Introduced in the late 1970s, the farming of red and green seaweed quickly expanded and took over as the primary source of income for mainly Lembongan and Ceningan. Farms were erected all along the coastlines, surrounding almost all of both islands in locations where there was consistent access to shallow, intertidal zones.

In 2014, there was a major shift in seaweed agriculture, where about 90% of the farmers transitioned to the tourism industry. This occurred not because tourism was flourishing and the income was substantially better, but more so due to a significant drop in the international price of seaweed. In 2014, 1 kilogram of dry red seaweed sold for 3,500 Rp, compared to a price of 12,000 to 14,000 IDR/kg dry seaweed in 2022. The only farms that remained were the ones located in the channel of Lembongan and Ceningan, used as an attraction for day tour companies.

As a result of the 2020 pandemic, international tourism in Indonesia declined severely. Thus sprouting a gradual shift back to local seaweed farming at the end of 2020, as a means of sustaining livelihood. This brings us to 2022, where seaweed farms are now at 60% capacity of what they used to be, prior to 2014, and the blossoming of a local empowerment movement; the Cube Seaweed Project.

From seed to harvest

Each local family in the seaweed farming business has plots in various locations around the islands, chosen according to the movement of the water and the nutrients it brings, tide difference, and seasons. From planting to harvest, the process of seaweed farming takes about 20 to 30 days, with an additional 3 to 4 days of drying. It usually consumes 8 to 9 hours per day of work, in between harvesting young and healthy plants for replanting,

photo: @earthafloat
TheIntenseCalm.com

and older weeds for drying during low tide, preparations for new lines, cleaning old lines, drying throughout the high tide, and replanting on the next low. Replanting occurs continuously until a family has reached their maximum plot capacity, so as to ensure a constant supply of seaweed. Only when the capacity is reached, will they harvest seaweed for drying and selling for product.

Green seaweed is mostly grown around the islands as it sells dry for more than red seaweed at 35,000Rp per kilogram. When dried, the seaweed is sold to buyers who send it to Bali. It is then brought to Java where it is distributed internationally, predominantly to China and Japan, where it is used by manufacturers in beauty products such as hand and body lotion, shampoo, soap, make up and perfume.

photo: @earthafloat
TheIntenseCalm.com

Heading towards the future, the project is looking at locally creating more variety in products that can be sold directly to individual consumers and can be stored for a longer amount of time.

What is the Cube?

Brought to life in 2022, the Cube Project was formed as a movement for creating a self sustainable regional economy which empowers local seaweed farmers. This is done by locally processing the seaweed into a product that can be sold directly, hence allowing healthy profits. The Cube with its team and volunteers helps to promote the seaweed products as well as setting up seaweed farming as a form of ecotourism on the islands. Thus helping farmers move up from the bottom of the global supply chain and dependency on international seaweed prices that fluctuates greatly and leaves paper thin margins for the farmers. The first product that came out of this program was a seaweed gel cube (hence the name) that restaurants put in their smoothie and call Good Karma Smoothie.

The method of producing seaweed cubes adds an additional 1 to 2 days of work, after the seaweed has dried. This includes rinsing the seaweed several times with freshwater, soaking it overnight, boiling the product with added ingredients such as spirulina, moringa and chlorella. The added components are what makes the cubes additionally healthy and nutritious, as well as creates the green color of the cubes. Once the mixture has been boiled, it is poured into a mould where it is left to harden overnight. On the following day, the cubes are cut, placed into jars and are stored or distributed as a product to restaurants which support the Cube Project.

At each restaurant, a signature health smoothie of their choice is created with the seaweed cubes, and sold as a drink called the 'Good Karma Smoothie'. The profits of the smoothie are split evenly between the farmer and the project. It's a program that not only creates direct social impact with proven 100+ profit for seaweed farmer per kg seaweed, it is also a project that is generating more sustainability the more it grows contributing to many positive things including carbon capture and nitrogen consumption.

IndoIslandHoppers.com : Nusa Lembongan

Below is a list of supporters on the islands who serve the Good Karma Smoothie. Be sure to check out these fantastic places and strengthen a sustainable local economy!

- Ombak Zero Waste Café
- Kayu Lembongan
- Fin Island
- Ginger and Jamu
- Pisang Pisang
- B'Fresh
- Alponte Restaurant
- Bali Eco Deli
- The Sampan
- Ohana's
- World Diving
- Batu Karang

Moving forward

The Good Karma Smoothie program is now moving over to the big brother island of Bali with the start in Ubud. Already some of the most popular restaurants in Ubud have started supporting the program, like Sayuris, Alchemy, Kafe and Pyramids of Chi. Hopefully more will follow.

Do you want to support the program? Right now the program is looking for help to expand in Bali and to employ a representative in Bali to implement the Good Karma Smoothie program in restaurants. There is also a focus group you can join to try new seaweed derived products and give feedback. Contact is most easily done through the programs instagram page where they give continuous updates on the progress of the program and their launch events: @ thecubeseaweed.

- Kayli Wouters

Community

photo: @earthafloat
TheIntenseCalm.com

OUTDOORS: DIVING

Robot Best / Nusa Lembongan surfer & surf instructor @robot_wayan
photo: @earthafloat TheIntenseCalm.com

SURF N SPORT

Komo Wilson / Nusa Lembongan surfer / surf instructor @komowilson
photo: @earthafloat TheIntenseCalm.com

SUNGAI WATCH

River Warriors

The Balinese way of life revolves around the philosophy of Tri Hita Karana, meaning the "3 causes of goodness". This is the understanding of the importance of harmony between humans, between humans and nature, and between humans and their creator. Thus, the pillars of Balinese living establishes a strong relationship base between the Balinese people and the living environment which surrounds them.

Sungai Watch

Water in Bali

Bali holds a strong agrarian history in which the role of water is central to soil fertility. Water is considered the giver of life, the foundation of prosperity, and is therefore revered throughout the island of Bali. This, along with the fusion of Hindu practices, local Balinese beliefs and cultural traditions has given way to Agama Hindu Bali (Balinese Hinduism), originally known as Agama Tirta, which translates to "The Religion of Holy Water".

There are various kinds of holy water and is used in many different types of rituals, daily offerings, and religious practices. Holy water is considered a physical medium for spiritual regeneration, something unseen, sacred and divine. It is prepared daily by priests, where it is infused with flowers, sacred mantras and mudras, and is treated with utmost respect.

Hence, the reverence of water in Bali has both practical and spiritual applications. Rituals using holy water serve to maintain the balance and harmony between the human body, mind, and heart. Whilst in farming and irrigation, water is held in high regard as it helps keep the tranquility and equilibrium between humans and the natural environment. Despite its high reverence, the waters within and surrounding Bali currently experience high levels of plastic pollution.

Plastic and the Living Nature

Being in the middle of rainy season here in Indonesia, you might be familiar with some of the shocking levels of plastic waste that wash up along the beautiful beaches of Bali. During the wet months of October to April, trash that has been littered or illegally dumped in unregistered land fills are pushed into waterways by heavy rainfall. It is then carried out into the ocean through rivers where some of it winds up on Indonesian coastlines, and the rest are brought out to sea by deep water currents.

Plastic can take hundreds of years to break down, and even then they will be scattered throughout our lands and seas as microscopic bits called micro-plastic, which can be just as, if not more harmful to the environment than larger pieces of plastic. Plastic in our natural environment for one thing, doesn't look good. It also impacts the integrity of the soil, releases harmful chemicals into the ground and water, harms animals as they can get stuck in certain pieces, and gets mistaken for food as well. In the form of micro-plastic, humans and animals both are more likely to accidentally consume these harmful products, whether it be mistaken for food or digested through the food chain. The chemicals that are used to make plastic are unsafe for humans and animals to ingest, and can have extremely detrimental effects on the living environment if left unmanaged.

According to recent studies done by a local environmental organization called Sungai Watch (translates to River Watch), Indonesia is ranked as the second largest plastic polluter of the oceans after China[1]. In Bali alone, only 4% of plastic waste is recycled[1]. This is due to minimal efforts for waste management along with a lack of recycling infrastructure and local incentive. These issues are driving a

Sungai Watch

constant increase in the number of illegal dumps on Bali, and therefore contributes to the growing amount of plastic pollution that is entering our valuable oceans..

Fighting for the Oceans

Thankfully, there are people out in the field in Bali who are working every day to solve this issue and clean up our island and our oceans. This is the aim of Sungai Watch. It is found that more than 80% of plastic waste in the oceans comes from rivers[1]. This is the underlying problem which Sungai Watch aims to put an end to. They describe themselves as; an environmental organization on a mission to stop plastic from entering the ocean. The main way that they do this is by designing simple trash barriers that are placed upstream in rivers, and are cleaned every day. The trash collected from these in-place barriers are then sorted at their facilities, analyzed, and up-cycled. Sungai Watch is also currently experimenting with new ways of turning trash into different reusable products!

Sungai Watch also conducts and organizes loads of outreach sessions and education campaigns to engage local communities in the issues of plastic pollution, and to encourage responsible waste management on the island of Bali. They also host presentations at schools and with the local government, along with weekly community clean ups in villages. In addition to these weekly clean ups, Sungai

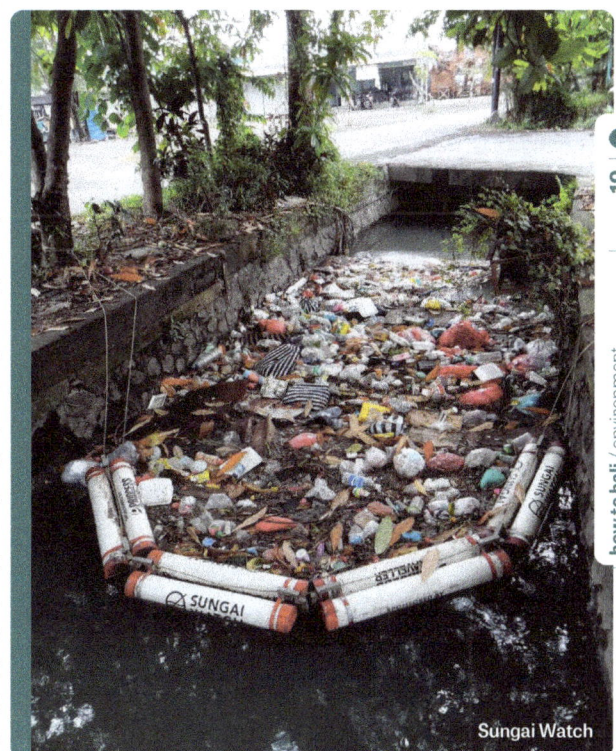
Sungai Watch

Watch also organizes emergency clean ups at illegal land fills, mainly alongside riverbanks in order to prevent plastic from entering the water in the first place.

Sungai Watch plans to place trash barriers in every river in Indonesia by 2025, and eventually become an international project and movement. How amazing is that?!

Get Involved with the Cause!

Want to know the ways in which YOU can get involved and help the cause? Here are some listed below;

• You can report illegal landfills and trash filled rivers in Bali and Indonesia to Sungai Watch via their hotline at +62 821-4781-382.

• You could help sponsor a community clean up, production and implementation of a river barrier, or trash dropbox in a local community in Bali.

• You can help organize a fundraiser in your school or community with outreach and education. The donations collected will go towards; hiring local people to collect and sort the waste, scouting for and cleaning areas, equipment, conducting waste audits, as well as organizing more events and campaigns.

• You can also simply volunteer at a weekly clean up. The information for these locations are listed on their website and updated regularly, along with further information on all the bits listed above at: www.sungaiwatch.com

- Kayli Wouters

Sungai Watch

Together with your help, we can clean up our island and restore the pristine waters in which Bali once held!

References
1. *River Warriors* (2022) *Sungai Watch*. Sungai Watch . Available at: https://sungai.watch/pages/about-us (Accessed: November 20, 2022)

photo Indhira Adhista
IG @raw_image6

Fertility and
Sustainability

A common theme that has run throughout this journal is the nutrient rich, fertile soil of Bali. The volcanic history that has taken place in order to create the Island of Gods has bestowed the Balinese with agricultural abundance.

Maukami

International visitors and influence has been rapidly increasing in Bali over the last decade. The stunning beaches, crystal clear waters, Jurassic-like wilderness and mountains have become more and more the ideal holiday destination for people traveling from all over the globe.

In the last two years, Bali has suffered particularly hard due to the effects of the corona virus on international travel. I say this because Bali relies a lot more on the tourism industry than most of the rest of Indonesia. Therefore, it is more important now than ever, as Bali recovers from its recent hardships and continues to expand its tourism industry, in order to preserve and maintain the essence of Balinese culture, to secure economic independence for the local people, and ensure environmental sustainability of their lands.

Of course, there are many different ways in which this can be done. What I am going to talk about now is how these issues can be tackled and how these aims can be acquired, through organizations aimed at education and development of sustainable agriculture.

Maukami

Maukami

Maukami

MAUKAMI

The first movement of which I will speak about is Maukami. Maukami works with Balinese farmers and villages to create sustainable living by which they are able to thrive and make the most of their land, whilst achieving financial independence. They promote self reliance and economic independence of the Balinese through empowerment by innovating methods for farming which revolve around traditional knowledge. Whilst innovating with the local community for sustainable and organic farms, kitchens, and crafts, Maukami supports Indonesians also by building fair trade models and mutually beneficial partnerships between farmers and the market through personal guidance and mentorship.

Located just outside of Canggu, you can take part in the experience that is the Maukami farm and kitchen. Here, you can learn about the sources of local organic food and the relationships between soil and plate as you participate in this process. This includes visiting the farm and picking the ingredients which you will be working with, using traditional Balinese methods and tools to prepare and cook the food, as well as making handicrafts using natural resources and materials. The entire process is undertaken with local Balinese farmers and villagers and is a wholesome experience which educates and supports communities in sustainable living, farming, and the value we should cherish and protect which is Bali's rich agricultural land.

Community

The Kul Kul Farm

Astungkara Way

Located in Sibang Kaja between Denpasar and Ubud is the Kul Kul farm. Here, permaculture, agroforestry, and regenerative agriculture are put into practice.

In brief terms, agroforestry is a form of agriculture that incorporates the cultivation of trees on their plot. This creates an ecologically diverse and resilient ecosystem. The intended idea of permaculture is to create agricultural ecosystems that are sustainable and self-sufficient. It is the designing of an ecologically sound way of living which encourages us to be resourceful and self-reliant.

Regenerative agriculture prioritises the care of our natural ecosystem. It's practice encompasses improving soil health by incorporating crop rotation and cover cropping, increasing plant and crop diversity to expand overall area biodiversity, managing rotational grazing and pasturing for livestock, integrating conservative tillage to prevent erosion, aid irrigation, and increase the overall health of the soil; all of which would support carbon sequestration. The more carbon that is sequestered into the earth instead of being released into our atmosphere can aid in our efforts of mitigating and combating climate change.

The Kul Kul farm has adopted these concepts and offers workshops in its practices. It also has a large focus on encouraging the younger generation - of Balinese and foreigners - to farm, in addition to working with local communities in providing farming jobs that are worthwhile. Much like Maukami, the Kul Kul farm aims to empower local people and their land in ways that are environmentally and economically sustainable, whilst educating everyone on the importance of sustainable agriculture.

Astungkara Way

Finally, we come now to Astungkara Way. This project also advocates for sustainability in local economy, community and ecosystems, through the practice of regenerative tourism as opposed to mass tourism.

Astungkara Way aims to connect you with your food, with nature and with the Balinese culture by providing experiences.

These include trips through the island of Bali where you will walk/hike trails through rice fields, mountains, and villages as you learn about the source of Balinese food, participate in farming activities with local Balinese farmers, discover hidden natural gems, connect with local families, and learn about Bali's rich heritage.

- Kayli Wouters

Astungkara Way

Ancient folklore portrays the island of Bali resting on the shell of a huge turtle called 'Bedawang Nala'. The ocean surrounding the island is seen as the home to spirits, many of them demonic, and the mountains of Bali are considered the thrones of Hindu gods. Hence, the turtle that the island sits on represents a balance between the good and evil beings of the world.

Community

At the Beach
Turtles in Bali

In Asia, turtles have long been revered as symbols of strength, wisdom, and good luck. These gentle creatures can live for decades, and their unique appearance has inspired a vast number of stories and legends. Sadly, turtles are in danger of becoming extinct due to the illegal wildlife trade, habitat loss, and pollution.

Traditional History

Bali is world-renowned for its beautiful beaches and vibrant culture, along with a variety of spectacular wildlife, including the sea turtle. Starring in traditional legends, symbolism, and used in ceremonies, the sea turtle plays a significant role in the core beliefs of Balinese Hindus.

In Bali, the turtle symbolises wisdom and longevity. For centuries, Balinese culture has been steeped in legend and mythology. The turtle plays an important role in these many different stories. In one particular legend, the island of Bali was created when two great turtles emerged from the sea and supported the island on their backs. In another famous tale, a turtle used their shell to protect a jewel which had fallen from the gods, and thus the island was gifted by the gods as recognition for the selflessness of the turtle.

It is also popularly told in legends that Bali rests on the shell of a giant turtle named Bedawang Nala, (translates to mythical giant turtle). This giant turtle is said to represent the balance between good and evil. The good is depicted by

Photo: Rossi Photography

photo: @earthafloat
TheIntenseCalm.com

the mountains of Bali, considered as the thrones of Hindu gods, and the evil as the oceans surrounding the island; home to demonic spirits.

Because the turtle has such an importance in the Balinese faith, they were also included in several sacrificial rituals. Green sea turtles in particular were beheaded and offered as sacrifices for rituals celebrating significant milestones in a person's life. This includes ceremonies for the three-month birthday of a child, teeth filing at the age of sixteen, marriages, and cremations. Offering the life of a sea turtle has been engrained over time, spiritually and culturally in the lives of local Balinese. Outside of religious traditions, sea turtle meat was also popularly offered to household guests as a custom to show a life of luxury.

Today, sea turtles are still revered by the people of Bali. They are often seen as a lucky charm, and used symbolically in temples and other sacred spaces.

Threatened Species

There are seven known sea turtle species in the world. Six of them inhabit the waters surrounding Bali and throughout Indonesia. These are;

- Green sea turtles
- Olive Ridley sea turtles
- Loggerhead sea turtles
- Flatback sea turtles
- Leatherback sea turtles
- Hawksbill sea turtles

Facing numerous threats of climate change, pollution, ocean acidification, biodiversity loss and degradation, our marine ecosystem relies not only on humans, but also on the organisms and animals that inhabit our oceans to combat these threats, and maintain a healthy ecological balance on our planet. Sea turtles in particular, maintain the health of coral reefs and sea grass habitats by feeding and foraging. Spending most of their lives in the ocean, they also contribute to enriching coastal ecosystems by coming to nest on beaches.

There are several beaches in Bali that are visited by sea turtles. These commonly consist of beaches lining Kuta, Medewi, Rambut Siwi, and Perancak. Most sea turtles will lay several groups of eggs called clutches, once every 2 to 4 years. Each clutch can contain between 100 to 200 eggs. In Bali, nesting season usually takes place between the months of March to September. Sea turtles mate and travel to the sandy beaches of Bali to lay their eggs. Once the eggs are laid, the female will cover them with sand and return to sea. They are not maternal animals and so the eggs will hatch after about two months, and the baby turtles will then make their way to the water on their own, and begin their life at sea. The population of sea turtles also contribute to the local economy as seeing them in the wild is a popular attraction for tourists. Thus, turtles have an important role to play in different areas of environmental and economic sustainability.

Despite their prominent influence, sea turtle populations are in decline. In 1999, the Indonesian government granted sea turtles a protected status. However, a black market still exists. Every year, turtles and their eggs are taken from the wild and sold illegally in Bali, across Indonesia, as well as internationally. Their body and eggs are bought for use in traditional medicine, their shell is used to craft souvenirs, jewellery, and other luxury items, their skin can be used for leather goods, and their oil in certain beauty products. Along with the effects of habitat loss, pollution, and urban development, sea turtle populations are threatened, with some species now critically endangered.

On Bali, the awareness of endangering sea turtles and the importance of maintaining a healthy population in the wild has improved significantly over the last few decades. Thus, it is becoming increasingly rare to find sea turtles at traditional rites and restaurants.

Awareness for Conservation

If you're interested in learning more about sea turtles, there are several conservation, rescue, and turtle education centres in Bali that you can visit. Whether it is to volunteer with general maintenance, participate in baby turtle releasings, or donate to the centre, there is a lot that can be done to help the sea turtles.

The Kurma Asih Sea Turtle Conservation Centre is located in the Jembrana Regency of Northwest Bali. At this centre, they focus on gathering wild nests from the beaches and caring for them in their nursery. Once the turtles have hatched and are about 6 months old, they are then released into the ocean. Kurma Asih also conducts research on sea turtles and care for the ones that were not strong enough to be released into the wild.

Another large conservation centre is the Turtle Conservation and Education Centre on Serangan Island. Created in 2006 by a former Bali governor, the centre also aids in releasing new hatchlings, in addition to nursing sick and injured turtles back to health. Furthermore, they also work to shut down the black market for sea turtle trade in Bali through educating and promoting awareness for conservation to the local population. One of the ways this is done is by providing sea turtles at ceremonies to be shown as living animals with intrinsic value.

Bali Sea Turtle Society (BSTS) is another movement for the conservation of sea turtles. Founded in 2011, BSTS is a non-profit NGO that aims to educate and work with local communities in Bali through community based conservation efforts such as nest protection, education and campaigning.

We need sea turtles for a sustainable marine environment, and they need our voice and support for conservation. Check out these centers and what you can do throughout your stay in Bali!

- Allison Moore

Loloh Cemcem

Ingredients (serves 8)

- Cemcem leaves
- Coconut water
- Young coconut meat
- 120gr or 8tbsp of tamarind
- 120gr or 8tbsp of sugar
- 1 tbsp of salt
- Pinch of shrimp paste
- Chili to taste.(1 pc)

How to make it:

1. Boil sliced chilies, shrimp paste, tamarind, sugar, and salt. Wait until you smell the fragrance.

2. Wash the cemcem leaves, then mash or knead them.

3. Mix the cemcem leaves into the boiled tamarind water. Wait until it changes color.

4. Turn off the stove and pour the water into a glass.

5. Add coconut water and coconut meat, and ice cubes to make it colder.

Bali, the most famous island in Indonesia, is known by its stunning nature and its unique hospitable culture. Bali has beautiful mountains, lakes, beaches, and waterfalls. Visitors can also enjoy a taste of Balinese culture everywhere in the island including ceremonies at the temples that cannot be found anywhere else in the world. Besides, Bali is also a famous destination for culinary tourists from all over the world looking for delicious and healthy dishes that Bali has to offer. One of those unique healthy Balinese drinks is Loloh Cemcem.

Loloh Cemcem is a traditional Balinese drink made from several types of plants and is produced by mostly small co-ops. The Balinese people have believed for generations that Loloh has great health benefits, and it is a popular drink among people who seek alternative natural remedies derived from plants. Loloh cemcem is a famous traditional drink in Penglipuran Village, and tourists who go there usually sample and buy the drink as a souvenir. In the Penglipuran Village area, there are 9 Loloh cemcem producers who continuously make the drink every morning. The shelf life of the Loloh Cemcem is still uncertain. From the results of interviews conducted by researchers with the producers of Loloh cemcem, it seems that it can last for 3 days (72 hours) in the refrigerator (1-4°C).

Loloh Cemcem has a very distinctive taste from other herbal medicines. Cemcem or kedondong leaves combined with other ingredients produce a unique taste that gives the drink a salty, sweet, spicy, and slightly sour taste. In addition to refreshing the body, Loloh Cemcem helps relieve heartburns, smooth constipation, and even lowers blood pressure. Even though Loloh Cemcem has a slightly sour taste, it is safe to drink on an empty stomach.

- Triana Ardi

For more local food, drinks & recipes, scan the QR CODE on the next page with your cell phone -- >

Signature Rolls

NORI
Bali

SCAN ME

LOCAL FOOD,
DRINK & RECIPES

eat & drink

Modern Batik

Oedel is a growing clothing and fashion name that was recently selected to host a booth at the G20 conference. It's a natural choice given the batik style. On the other hand, Oedel applies a contemporary and modern touch to batik tradition. HowToBali caught up with owner and designer, Theresia. She is an Indonesian local who has travelled and lived around the world. She returned to Indonesia, to build her brand and establish a base in Bali. We wanted to ask her how she has arrived to the present and what the future may bring.

HowToBali: Hi! ..thank you for talking to us. When did you first dream of starting your own brand?

Theresia: I first dreamt of having my own brand when I was solo traveling in Europe. I traveled 7 countries and when I was in Belgium, I saw a bunch of lovely shops there with beautiful fashion. Then there was a voice in my head saying; 'what if there was another fashion store, but with a Batik concept?' I was captivated by the possibility of showcasing Indonesian culture in another land.

HowToBali: How long from then to the time you put logo and label on your first product, and what was that product?

Theresia: After my travels in Europe, I came back to Indonesia and I decided to move to Bali, an international hub, and create a cultural clothing line there. I wanted Indonesian Batik to be taken to other countries. It took 5 months until I put my logo onto my first product on the island of paradise. That first product was women's top wear. It showed Oedel (navel) as an expression of freedom in style with cultural blends.

HowToBali: What has been the reaction from people new to Batik style?

Theresia: Foreign tourists admire the beautiful Indonesian Batik motifs, and are especially intrigued with the traditional process of making the Batik using hot wax. Not only is it interesting to really observe the individual motifs, but in every stroke of the motif there is a story or history.

HowToBali: What feedback has interested you the most?

Theresia: Feedback that I have gotten from several regular customers which interests me the most is that they love the unique Batik style of Oedel. They mentioned that getting the right kind of Batik was difficult but in Oedel, they found many pieces of interest as it transforms Indonesian culture into something trendy and stylish.

HowToBali: What local designers and early experience inspired you about Batik?

Theresia: My late grandmother lived in Pekalongan, the City of Batik, so I was exposed to stories and beautiful Batik motifs from a very early age. In my childhood I also lived in Salatiga, which is an hour away from Solo, which is also a city famous for its Batik work. There I learned to make Batik and appreciate the Indonesian Culture even more. From then on, I was inspired to preserve Batik, and to share stories through Batik motifs to the world.

HowToBali: In what ways have local Indonesians reacted and commented on your designs?

Theresia: The reactions of local Indonesian tourists and visitors is first, usually laughter. This is because the word "Oedel" is eye-catching and brings curiosity about the brand name itself which is another word for navel, or belly button. They feel that Oedel's Batik work is beautiful and unique. Not only in the choice of colorful motifs, but also in the display of modernity in each of its models. The models that Oedel works with really understand and respect the traditional themes of Batik that are here being used in a contemporary and cool way.

Oedel Fashion

HowToBali: How did you get involved with the G20 event?

Theresia: Basically, I got an invitation from a friend who is active in "state activities". The first time I came to Bali and started the Batik brand Oedel, I didn't know anyone or of any events that I could join to help promote Oedel. So, I went around Bali to look for events like bazaars, weekend and weekday markets. I visited Canggu, Sanur, Uluwatu and other popular ends of Bali. From these travels I made new connections and friends who were going through a similar process of their own. And thus, we continued along this path together. One of the connections that I made on these trips was the multi-talented Meity. Meity often took part in state events, and was the one who introduced me to the G20 committee, and together we were invited to have a spot in the G20 event at the Nusa Dua Markets.

HowToBali: How was the experience and what other interesting booths were there?

Theresia: The euphoria of joining this world event in Bali, Indonesia was huge and I feel so happy and proud! There were so many booths that were interesting! There were lots of extraordinary and handmade creations by Indonesian people. I also saw something new and cool which were the booths for electric motorbikes, cars and buses with futuristic designs. There was also a variety of traditional food available. All sides of the market had interesting and unique stands which were attended by various ministers and guests of the country.

HowToBali: How do you see Oedel evolving in the coming year and years?

Theresia: From year to year, Oedel learns to understand more of what the customers want. I think that I'm slowly moving towards making custom pieces with stories and art that are specific to customers and each order. An example of this evolution is when I made a special event outfit for Tasya Karissa, a co-founder of Biorock. This event which she attended was held by the AIS (Archipelagic and Island States) Forum. There, she spoke in front of 46 international country delegates about solutions for the issues facing the world's oceans. And so, the designs that I created for her offered stories from the batik motif; sea waves. My current collection can be found at Bintang Supermarket in Ubud and Seminyak.

Interviewed by Thirumoolar Devar

oedel.id

Old School, New Blood

The word "Legend," can refer to both, the living for which stories are told, and also, the eternal stories which live for the generations. As with technology and evolution, our application of tools and knowledge is a layered experience of the legends who've paved the way for us. How one reacts to the changing tides; the ebb and flow of life's journey is what makes legends. Through them, we learn about the tenacity required to realize our dreams.

Born in 1954, legendary surfboard shaper, Bruce Hansel's passion for surfing was cultivated in the transitional days of the shortboard revolution. After stints in California, Mexico, and El Salvador, he earned notoriety on Northshore Hawaii's world-famous Pipeline. After yearly trips to Indonesia he made it home in 1999. He started a legal registered business importing blanks and materials from Australia and to this day lives his dream of handcrafting custom boards in Bali. Bruce's daughter, Cinta Hansel, is a local surfing champion. She's already carved a few legends into the waves of time herself!

HowToBali talked with the Bruce Hansel to illuminate a little upon the journey to today, still making custom surfboards and still making new legends...

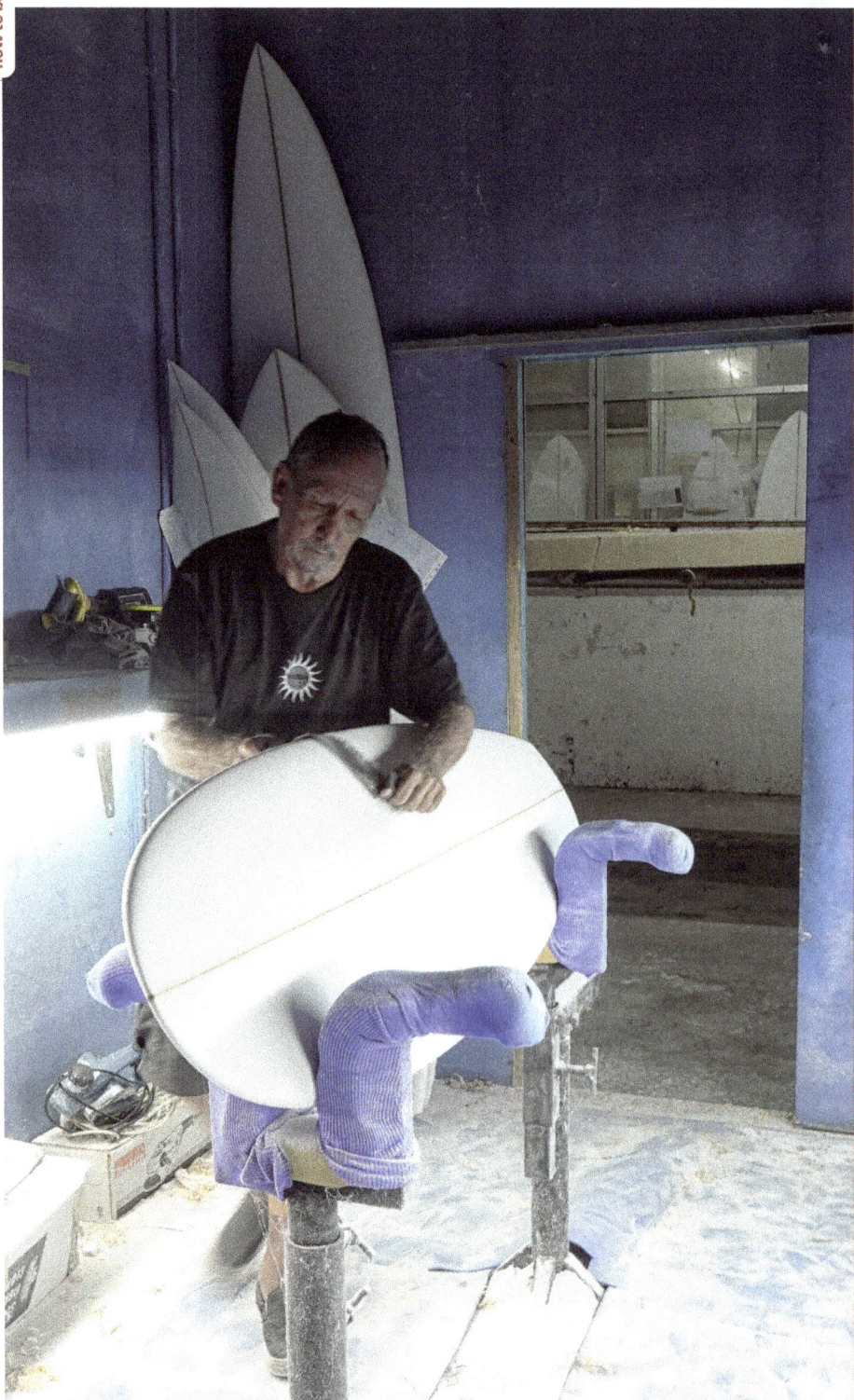

HowToBali: Where did you start surfing?

BH: I started surfing on the Gulf Coast of Florida. But I would often get rides with the older crew to go surf East Coast. And when I was 12 years old, I started to spend the summers with my dad in Satellite Beach, Florida which is south of Coco Beach. My surfing advanced dramatically after that first summer. And in the winters I was so hungry for surf I would hitchhike 100 miles across the state to surf for the weekend! Gnarly! LOL!!

HowToBali: ..and thus began an illustrius career in surfing?

BH: I started competition on the Gulf Coast of Florida at Holmes Beach (North of Sarasota) in 1969 and got 3rd in my age division. In 1970, I got 2nd. I competed for years in Coco Beach while staying with my dad in summer times, and my mom would take me on spring break to compete in Coco Beach and we would camp out!

In 1976 I got recognized for advancing 3 heats by the local magazine, Waverider. They printed my photo in a small barrel and about how I hitchhiked 100 miles to be in the competition!!!

I went to Hawaii in 1979 and entered the pro-class trials at Sunset Beach. Day one was too big for Sunset and it moved to 15"+ Haleiwa! I won 2 heats and advanced to the quarter-finals back at 10-12" Sunset. I lost my heat, but for a Florida rookie, my new Hawaiian friends were blown away.

After the pro-class trials, I wanted to compete in the Pipe Masters. I sent Randy Rarick an intro letter asking how I could get in. He arranged a meeting with me and told me he wanted me to surf for and represent Hawaii in the Pipe Masters. I wanted to represent Florida. He said, "no. If I'm gonna put you in, you're representing Hawaii." I said, "...but, I'm gonna get my ass kicked. I just arrived here. I'm from Florida." He goes, "na, you're protected." I found out later, yeah - I was protected. ...by the Black Shorts!!

He also told me I needed to go back East to compete and get points to qualify in the IPS (the original organization before the ASP and WSL). I first had a comp in New Jersey. I bombed out! From New Jersey I got a ride to Florida, my home state. The comp would be held at Sebastian Inlet. But the hurricane blew through and blocked the road with downed trees and the comp got held at Canaveral Pier in 1 foot slop. Anyway, I was riding a twin-fin, shaped by Cort Gion, which really helped me surf

Bruce Hansel at Padang Padang for Surfers Journal
photo: Don King

such small waves. I was hanging out with the Hawaiian guys, because I already knew them! So, they call me over, and I end up in a car with Michael Ho, Dane Kealoha, and Buttons. Me and Michael were gonna have our man on man heat together because I got into the main event. All I needed to do was compete in that heat. I didn't even need to win. I said, "hey Michael, c'mon man, you're not even gonna compete the whole comp - you're going back to California tonight" (because the swell hit there), and he's laughing and said, "yeah, but I'm still gonna kick your ass." He did... well... sorta... I mean... we battled. Anyway, that heat with Michael put me into the Pipe Masters. It was front page news in Cocoa Beach; that I advanced to the main event.

Peter Townend came up and congratulated me and told me Rarick had called from Hawaii to say; I was in the Pipe Masters, representing Hawaii. I was protected by The Hui! I was 23 years old. I got invited to the Pipe Masters 4 times.

HowToBali: What was the feeling of having a magazine shot at Pipe "back in the day?

BH: It's a lot different, because not so many photos came out all the time like now in the digital age. You only got a chance to get featured in a magazine and the major ones were *Surfer* or *Surfing*. So, if you got in there you were really somebody! And if you continued to get in there, you're definitely somebody! I had a couple shots in the bag back in Florida. When I flew to live in Hawaii, I'd only been there maybe 4 or 5 months and I'm working in the health food store bagging up the bulk food. A friend of mine walks in and just opens the magazine to the centerfold; it's me in the barrel at Pipeline, but they had the wrong name on the photo. So, I had to write a letter to the magazine and correct them. They published the correction. Yeah, it was a lot different. It meant a lot more. Now, anybody and everybody can post their photos. Back then, no! You couldn't do that! You only got what you got, and you were only who you were! You couldn't make yourself somebody that you're not, kinda like people do nowadays. We were the Pipeline Underground. And we became the Pipeline Underground because of *Surfer Magazine*. They ran our photos and they called us that. Another year, I'm at my house at Rocky Point, and Jeff Divine, a photographer for *Surfer Magazine*; he comes over to my house and walks up and opens up the magazine - shows me this giant wave at Second Reef of me doing a bottom turn getting ready to pull into the barrel. He goes, "hey, waddya you think about that?" I said, "wow! That's crazy." He goes, "yeah, but wait a minute; read the caption." The caption was, "Bruce Hansel, the vanguard of the Pipeline Underground." This was about 2 or 3 years after the Pipeline Underground had been named by *Surfer Magazine*. I was like, "what!?!" I'm trippin, I'm from Florida and you guys are calling me the head of the Pipeline Underground now? It was crazy. Yeah.

But it's great to see Cinta get all her coverage and in the online magazines and stuff. Yeah, it's great!

Cinta Hansel
photo: @oscrjms_

Cinta Hansel
photo: Billabong Asia

HowToBali: When did you move to Bali?

BH: I arrived in Bali to live permanently in 1999, after surfing in Bali every year for 2-3 months since 1981. My first daughter was born with cerebral palsy and I wanted to move to Bali with my Indonesian wife so we could have family to help with our daughter. My plan was to start a Surfboard Business. I created a logo called "Indo Ski" and promoting it while still in Hawaii. I was already riding the boards in Bali and G-Land etc., with great success and compliments from Gerry Lopez and Dennis Pang.

HowToBali: So, you left the world's most iconic surf spot, the Banzai Pipeline, and then you're at the newly discovered and also notorious, Balinese pipeline, Padang Padang?

BH: It was incredible, the waves, the people, everything. My experience was a bit different. Straight away, my board carrier saw how much I liked to surf from the morning all the way through the day until the evening. I'd go ride my motorbike back to Kuta in the dark. One day he said, "hey Bruce you already know the waves are good on the full moon and the new moon." I said, "yeah, I know that." He said, "you know you're always welcome to stay at my house. We can bring you cold beer back from the warung and we'll get a chicken and we got vegetables and rice and you can eat dinner. You just give us a little bit for the chicken.." And so I did. I took him up on it. As soon as I did it one time, I did it every moon. I would stay at Uluwatu for two or three days, two days after the moon. I mean, before swell predictions, forecast, and all that; you just knew by the moon that the swell was gonna come on the moon. I kept trying to get my friends; it would get a bit boring and lonely out there... and in the mornings I'd be surfing by myself. In the evenings I'd be surfing almost

nobody out. I'd get Outside Corner and Padang in the same day. I would surf Outside Corner in the morning, Padang during the day and back to Outside Corner in the evening. You know, like, how can you beat that? I could never get -not one of my friends ever took me up on it. I mean, yeah, so my experience was different from a lot of people. I stayed at Uluwatu on the moons!

Padang Padang was great when it was uncrowded. But as soon as they built that bridge connecting Uluwatu to Padang.. You didn't have to walk down there anymore and then they paved the road down there and you didn't have to drive down that bumpy limestone road anymore. I preferred to walk from Uluwatu

anyway. But then it was over. All the locals wanted to surf it more than ever. They all wanted to get in the magazine or videos. It became a very competitive vibe out there. They'd still give me waves, but I just got over it. I just kept surfing Outside Corner more than Padang after that.

HowToBali: How did you originally get into shaping?

BH: Technically, I shaped my first surfboard in 1967. I saw the latest Surfer Magazine with the Shortboard Revolution starting. It was written that surfers in Australia were starting to strip the fiberglass off their longboards and cut them down to 8'0'' and shorter. I watched the World

Titles held in Puerto Rico and saw Wayne Lynch and Reno Abellira riding boards shorter than 7'0"! They were the best Surfers in the water but didn't win! The fire was sparked! I went to the Local Bait and Tackle Shop where my first 2 Longboards were bought, but they had nothing new. I walked in the back to watch a guy doing ding repair and saw him using a grinder and a small sander! I looked through the store and found a roll of fibreglass and resin. To make a long story short I went home and chopped my 9'6" board down to 6'10", and when I was having trouble with glassing before the resin went off my mom jumped in to help finish!!! I went surfing about 3 days later and got 3 orders when I went to the beach! I recruited my 2 best friends Chris Lundy and Kevin Stecker to help and we formed a backyard surfboard company called Metamorphosis with a butterfly logo, taken from the Iron Butterfly album by the same name!

So, I was shaping at 12 years old for 4 years, until I was 16. Then I was getting sponsored by a shop to ride major brands from California. I rode boards shaped by Cort Gion for most of the time. When Cort moved to Oregon I started riding for Eric Arakawa on his B-Team in Hawaii. After the birth of my first child, I started shaping again at 41 years old. I went and bought all the tools needed to start shaping again. That would be 1995. I was working at Bill Barnfield's factory in Haleiwa and working for Arakawa, airbrushing. I had just shaped my first board and put it in the stand-up racks waiting for glassing. I had signed it #1. And I came out of my room to see Dave Parmenter handling my board and fully checking it out! He spotted me and asked "really, number one???" I answered "yes, after 25 years and not shaping much before then ..." He said, "well don't STOP! I've seen guys shape 200 boards and nowhere close to as good as this!!! And shaping has changed since you stopped. This is excellent!"

Cinta gives me feedback about her boards, all the time. That's one of the reasons why my boards have gotten so good over the years, is because of her. She's really good on giving feedback. She's smart about her boards, and tells me what the feeling is here and there and whatever.

HowToBali: How does the competition part of your surfing experience fit juxtaposed to "soul surfing?"

BH: I'm always a "soul surfer", when I'm not competing, but I'm very competitive. I couldn't live without competing! I've competed nearly my entire surfing life! Even when I retired from competing at Pipeline, I'd still enter competitions here and there. If something came up, I couldn't help myself; I'd compete. I'm a competitor.

It's great seeing Cinta wanna compete. In the beginning I told her not to. I told her she would hate it, and it's a horrible feeling when you lose. But, she thrives off of it just like I did. She can't help herself. She wants to compete! When she asked me to compete and I took her for her first competition, yeah that was it. Game on! Never stopped, Kept going. She's had her ups and downs with injuries and bad judging and bad calls by the surfing organizations or whatever. And it really puts her down but she can't help herself. When she gets a chance to compete, there she is; she's competing again!

Interview & shop photos by Thirumoolar Devar

Bruce Hansel
photo: Don King

Bruce Hansel
photo: Ralph Cippola

Bruce Hansel
photo: Mike Waggoner / Surfer Magazine

Cinta Hansel
photo: unknown

Handcrafted Surf Boards
by

HANSEL
Hi-Performance

Surf's Up!!

- How much money is enough money?, 2021

About WD

WD (Wild Drawing) was born and raised on Bali Indonesia and has degrees in both Fine Arts and Applied Arts. He started painting in the street in 2000 and since then he spends most of his time working there, although he never stopped working in his studio too. WD has participated in festivals and exhibitions in Asia, Europe and the Americas while his work is featured in Street Art books worldwide.

His EastWest sociocultural background is combined in a unique way that makes his style particularly recognizable. WD focuses on large-scale murals created with roller brushes and acrylic paints, and always interacts with the spot where he is working by incorporating various elements of it into his work, so there is harmony between the mural and the spot where it was painted. His work - 3D anamorphic with optical illusions - is influenced by Comics, Graphic Novels and Fantastic Art, while he mainly gets inspired by social phenomena, lifestyle, art or nature.

What he loves most about painting

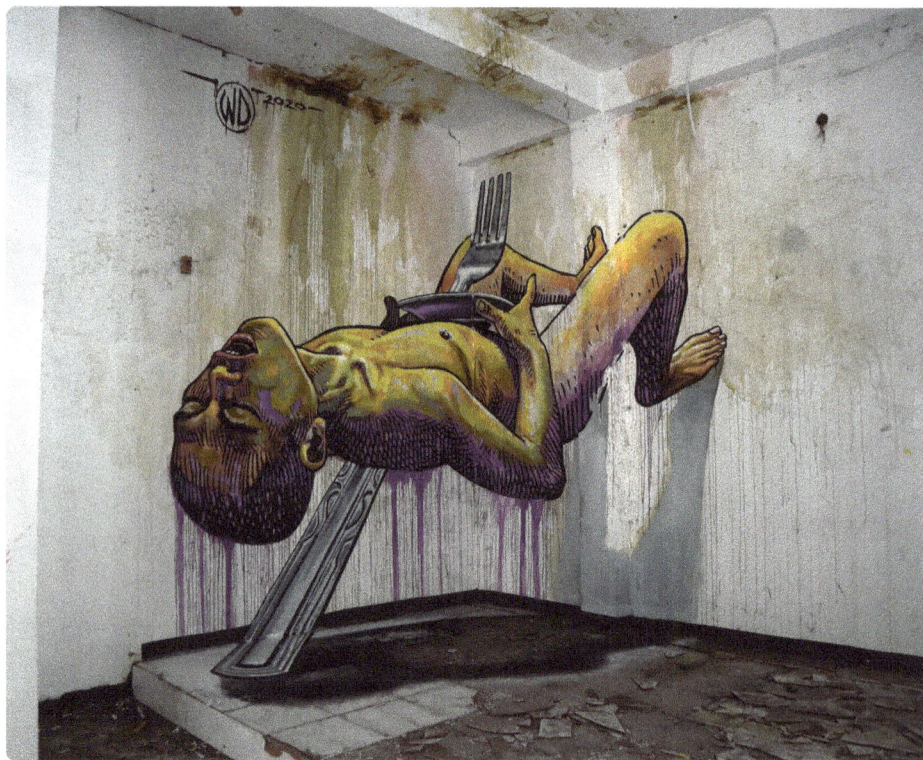

- Covid-19 vs Poverty, 2020

- Owlself, 2015

in the street is the unique freedom of expression and the fact that Street Art is freely accessed by everyone without social, economic, cultural or other limitations. Moreover through his art has the chance to speak about the big issue of the re-appropriation of Public Space. All this offsets the ephemeral nature of his art. After all, if he was interested in making artworks that stand the test of time he would do canvas paintings only. WD is currently based in Athens, Greece.

More about the artist:

instagram.com/wd_wilddrawing

facebook.com/wd.street.art

youtube.com/channel/
UC00eyhZ16VjnFasQ05VXV8Q

- Message, 2020

how to bali / street art

Doors @ Kesari

TUGU APIT LAWANG

Doors by Design

Architecture notoriously ornate suggest both attitude and humility at once. There is something to be said to a culture's ability to transcend basic survival pursuit. In that light an expression and creation rebounds, refracts, returns the mirth of existence to whence it originated.

In this vein, fascination of art and function compliment each other perfectly.

photos: TheIntenseCalm.com

TUGU APIT LAWANG

Bali Mantap

EcoArts

BIRTH OF AN ISLAND

KARMA CUBED

OLD SCHOOL NEW BLOOD

PORTAL OF EMBARKATION

Batik Modern

Cokelat Organik

Seni Jalanan

This publication is available in alternate languages and formats

Earth Afloat!

Magazine

fabled photos

THE INTENSE CALM

Awesome Photos

Kandui Villas

Mentawai Luxury Surf Resort

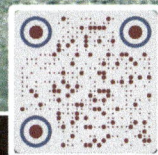

baby steps

Photos taken in Sept. 2021 ins a remote jungle village in East-Bali for a baby's 1-year old birthday ceremony by Thirumoolar Devar TheIntenseCalm.com

foto: Potret Pura Luhur Uluwatu 1930

Vintage Kecak

foto: EFD (Bali), [1935]

Portal of Embarkation

illustration: Ngurah Yudha
story & coloring: Thirumoolar Devar

Bali contribution
Agung Tattoos

WELCOME TO THE ASTRAL-THREAD SHUTTLE-BUS. DO YOU HAVE A DESTINATION IN MIND OR JUST ALONG FOR THE RIDE?

HUH!?! *SAY WHAT?*

YES, SIR. WE'RE ON A TRAIN AROUND THE EARTHS AFLOATING, PROPPELLED BY ENERGY WAVES. THE ENERGY WAVES ARE GUIDED BY MAGNETIC GRAVITY

www.ingramcontent.com/pod-product-compliance
Lightning Source LLC
Chambersburg PA
CBHW061012030426
42337CB00031B/5135